ACKNOWLEDGEMENTS

My students in the Heard Enrichment Program (HEP) in Heard County, Georgia, have been of immeasurable help in preparing and polishing *Create Heroes and Villains: Writing an Adventure Story*. They have been willing "guinea pigs" as I have tried out all the various activities in the unit on them over the past few years. Thank you, HEP students!

ABOUT THE COVER

The cover illustration depicts the destruction of the Chimera by the young Corinthian prince Bellerophon. According to ancient Greek mythology, the Chimera was a fire-breathing monster who had terrorized the people of Lycia; it was half lion and half goat and had a serpent tail. Asked by the king of Lycia to kill the Chimera, Bellerophon attacked the monster from the back of the winged horse Pegasus and was successful in destroying it.

Contents

ACKNOWLEDGEMENTS 3
INTRODUCTION TO THE TEACHER 7–9

HEROES AND SHEROES
Activity No. 1 What is a Hero? 12

SUPER HEROES /SHEROES
Activity No. 2 Definition of Super Hero/Shero 14
Activity No. 3 Characteristics 16
Activity No. 4 Values 18
Activity No. 5 Tools of the Trade 20
Activity No. 6 Strengths and Weaknesses 22
Activity No. 7 Problems and Crises 24
Activity No. 8 Super Villains 26
Activity No. 9 Writing the Story 28
Activity No. 10 Prepackaged Super Sheroes 30

FOLK HEROES
Activity No. 11 Definition of Folk Hero 32
Activity No. 12 Occupations and Values 34
Activity No. 13 Characteristics 36
Activity No. 14 Strengths and Weaknesses 38
Activity No. 15 Villains 40
Activity No. 16 Using Humor: Writing a Tall Tale 42
Activity No. 17 Suzy Stacks: A Trucking Shero 44

MYTHOLOGICAL HEROES
Activity No. 18 The Mythological Hero 46
Activity No. 19 The Monster as Villain 48
Activity No. 20 Write a Heroic Tale 50

OTHER WAYS TO USE A HERO
Activity No. 21 Other Ways to Use a Hero 52
Activity No. 22 Group-Created Stories 54
Activity No. 23 A Grab Bag of Suggestions 55

TEAR-OUT REPRODUCIBLE STUDENT WORK PAGES 57–80

NOTE: A duplicate set of student worksheet pages is provided. These perforated pages, which appear at the back of the book, may be detached for photocopying for use by the buyer in the classroom. This allows the teacher to keep the set of Teacher Directions and Student Pages side by side in the book.

INTRODUCTION TO THE TEACHER

Introduction to the Teacher

Students like to create, write, and share stories; however, they can be baffled and become resentful when told to write a short story without being shown how to write one. Not knowing where nor how to begin, much less how to develop and end, they often write one skimpy paragraph and call it a short story. Conversely, when they are led through the structure of a story step by step, they often surprise themselves with the results.

Wise teachers capitalize on popular culture in the classroom. They begin with what is already familiar and interesting to students and use that knowledge and interest as springboards to introduce new knowledge. *Create Heroes and Villains: Writing an Adventure Story* builds on the existing knowledge of and interest in super heroes, folk heroes, villains, mythological and legendary heroes, and monsters.

Heroes and heroines are always of special interest to students. Styles in heroes and heroines might change, but heroes and heroines never go out of style. They develop all over the world and at all levels of civilization. During Classic times heroes were god-men; during the Middle Ages heroes were God's men; the Renaissance period heroized universal men; gentlemen in the eighteenth century and self-made men in the nineteenth century were admired. Today, we list among our heroes and heroines the underdog, the outsider, the common man, athletes, rock stars, astronauts, and scientists.

Hero worship satisfies a special hunger in the human heart; it meets a deep psychological need. Heroes and heroines lose some of their humaness and become mirrors held up to a culture, reflecting the time and the place in which they live and the people's innermost hopes, values, and beliefs. The kinds of heroes or heroines a culture reveres reveals the values and purposes of that culture.

Children can write—some better than others, of course, but they all have the raw materials needed for creative writing floating around in their lives. *Create Heroes and Villains* is designed to bring order to those raw materials, help students sort and arrange that which is already familiar, and use the results to create stories. In the process of creating their stories, students will examine, discuss, and learn many new concepts. The by-products can be as rewarding as the finished stories.

Teachers will readily see that *Create Heroes and Villains* may be used as a creative-writing unit or in conjunction with a literature unit on heroes and heroines. Either way, teachers using the unit will need to read aloud to students (or assign them to read) appropriate literature to generate interest and discussion. With only a few modifications, it can be used with grades 4 through 12.

Create Heroes and Villains will help develop students' abilities in observing, concluding, recalling, applying, analyzing, synthesizing, evaluating, divergent thinking, and convergent thinking. At the same time it will contribute to the development of their oral, written, and imaginative skills, with the additional advantage of being fun. Finally, it can give students a final product of which they can be proud!

The unit is designed to save thinking time and preparation time for teachers and to encourage planned creativity. Some teachers neither need nor want minute descriptions of teaching approaches and objectives while other teachers, because of time limitations, need more detailed instructions. All are capable of modifying an idea to suit their own purposes and most prefer to innovate rather than copy. Therefore, teachers may use *Create Heroes and Villains* any way they wish, only their imaginations limiting the various possibilities.

Create Heroes and Villains is divided into four parts. The first part, comprising Activity No. 1 through Activity No. 10, is sequential, building up to the writing of an adventure story featuring super heroes/sheroes. The second part, comprising Activity No. 11 through Activity No. 17, follows a similar format with folk heroes/sheroes. The third part, which includes Activity No. 18 through Activity No. 20, deals with mythological heroes/sheroes. Detailed teacher directions are given for each activity, with several options suggested for additional consideration. The last section, comprising Activity No. 21 through Activity No. 23, simply offers additional choices. These last three activities may be used in many different ways, some of which are suggested in the teacher's directions at the beginning of the last section.

Behavioral objectives are not included as they are too precise and lengthy to include in a teaching unit of this type. No bibliography of suggested fiction is included because a quick trip to a library will yield sufficient information. Only a few examples are included because teachers will need to vary their examples depending upon the ages and abilities of their students.

I sincerely hope that *Create Heroes and Villains* will be as educational and as much fun for other teachers and students as it has been for my students and me.

Good luck!

CREATE HEROES AND VILLAINS

What Is a Hero?

Activity No. 1 **Teacher Directions**

Objectives: To introduce students to the concept of heroism

To help students to understand that the words "hero" and "heroine" have several different but related meanings

To encourage students to analyze their definitions of "hero" and "heroine" and to encourage them to broaden their definitions

Thinking Skills: Recall

Application

Analysis

Divergent Thinking

Evaluation

Directions: Discuss the following: What is a hero/heroine? Who is your favorite hero/heroine who actually lived? Is he or she living now? Why is he or she your favorite? Who is your favorite fictional hero/heroine? Why?

Tell the students: In this unit on heroes and heroines, we are going to create three major types of heroes/heroines—super heroes/heroines, folk heroes/heroines, and mythological heroes/heroines—and write stories about them. These three types of heroes/heroines evolved differently but for the same reasons. Mythological heroes/heroines and most folk heroes/heroines are rooted in oral stories while super heroes/heroines are literary inventions. All three types serve to mirror the time and place where they live and they reflect people's most innermost hopes and beliefs; they are symbols of what people admire most.

Discuss each of the six definitions of hero/heroine. Fill in the bottom half of Activity No. 1 as a group, discussing each choice and why it fits the definition.

Options: Other definitions of hero/heroine

What Is a Hero?

Activity No. 1

Student Work Sheet

There are many definitions of hero and heroine. Some of the most commonly accepted are listed below:

1. A hero/heroine is a person admired for his/her achievements and outstanding character.

2. A hero/heroine is a person who shows great courage.

3. A hero/heroine is the main character in a dramatic or literary work.

4. A hero/heroine is the central figure in an event or historical period.

5. A hero/heroine is an illustrious warrior.

6. A hero/heroine is a mythological or legendary figure, often of half-divine descent, endowed with extraordinary strength and/or ability.

List heroes and heroines who fit the above definitions. Be able to defend your choices.

HEROES	**HEROINES**
_____	_____
_____	_____
_____	_____
_____	_____
_____	_____
_____	_____

Definition of Super Hero/Shero

Activity No. 2   **Teacher Directions**

Objectives: To help students gain a working knowledge of super hero/shero

To assist students in defining super powers and discriminating among "physical," "mental," and "moral" powers.

To engage students in the creation of super powers for their super heroes/sheroes

Thinking Skills: Observation

Recall

Application

Analysis

Divergent Thinking

Convergent Thinking

Synthesis

Evaluation

Directions: Discuss the following: What is a super hero/shero? Shero is a made-up word. Why is it appropriate? Who is your favorite super hero/shero? Why? What special powers does he/she have? How does he/she use those powers?

Make sure that students understand that without special super power(s) a hero/shero is not super. Also make sure that they understand that these super powers must be used to benefit mankind! Have students fill out Activity No. 2 individually. Share orally, discussing the repercussions of each choice.

Options: Super heroes/sheroes as literary inventions

Comic books

Definition of Super Hero/Shero

Activity No. 2   **Student Work Sheet**

A super hero/shero is larger than life. He/she will usually be superior in many ways to the ordinary person. First of all, he/she must have at least one super power; sometimes he/she has several super powers. These super powers may be physical, mental, or moral. Whatever these super powers are, they must be used to benefit mankind! Below list six super powers that your created super hero/shero might possess. Think beyond the obvious physical powers. How can these powers be used to benefit mankind?

      POWER   **TYPE AND USES**

1. _____   _____
2. _____   _____
3. _____   _____
4. _____   _____
5. _____   _____
6. _____   _____

Now choose two of the above for your super hero/shero.

1. _____
2. _____

Explain why you chose those two.

1. _____
_____

2. _____
_____

Educational Impressions, Inc   Create Heroes and Villains

Characteristics

Activity No. 3 **Teacher Directions**

Objectives:
To assist students in understanding factors which make up the total person

To provoke students to question initial reactions to people based on superficial qualities

To guide students in selecting component parts for their super hero/shero

Thinking Skills:
Recall

Application

Analysis

Synthesis

Evaluation

Directions:
Discuss the following: What is the sex, ethnic background, and age of your favorite super hero/shero? In what ways do his/her sex, ethnic background, and age affect the way the other characters respond to him/her? How do they affect the way readers respond to him/her?

Lead students to an understanding of how various characteristics have either positive or negative effects and that not all people view a given characteristic in the same light. Have students create two names for their super heroes/sheroes—an undercover name (Diana Prince) and a super hero/shero name (Wonder Woman). Ask them to determine the age, ethnic background, age, religion, geographical origin (if appropriate), and physical characteristics. Also have them design everyday undercover clothes and a super costume with a symbol.

Options:
Stereotypes

Super sheroes

Other minority super heroes/sheroes

Symbols

16 *Create Heroes and Villains*   Educational Impressions, Inc.

Characteristics

Activity No. 3 **Student Work Sheet**

The sex, age, ethnic background, religion, dress, geographical origin, looks, and even name of your super hero/shero determine how the public views him/her. These factors also help determine how the super hero/shero behaves. Think through what you want your super hero/shero to be or do before you determine each factor below.

Undercover name & occupation _____

Super hero/shero name _____

Age _____   Ethnic background _____

Religion _____

Geographical origin: _____

Looks:

    Height _____

    Weight _____

    Build _____

    Hair Color _____

    Eye Color _____

Everyday dress _____

_____

_____

_____

Costume with symbol _____

_____

_____

_____

Values

Activity No. 4 **Teacher Directions**

Objectives: To provide an atmosphere wherein students may openly examine and discuss values

To encourage students to reason and project the consequences of certain choices

To engage students in developing worthwhile values for their super heroes/sheroes

Thinking Skills: Application

Analysis

Divergent Thinking

Convergent Thinking

Synthesis

Evaluation

Directions: Discuss the following: What are some of the values held by your favorite super hero/shero? Do you consider those values to be worthwhile? Explain. Do the values held by your favorite super hero/shero help or hinder him/her in "working for the good of mankind"? Explain. How do the values held by your favorite super hero/shero affect the decisions made by him/her?

Arrive at a working definition of "values." Guide students in understanding that what people value determines the decisions they make and the action they take. Have students fill out Activity No. 4 individually. Share the highest ranked values and the projected consequences of holding those values.

Options: Decision-making

How peers affect values of students

How culture helps determine values

Values

Activity No. 4   Student Work Sheet

Super heroes/sheroes hold certain values. A super hero/shero may value honesty or loyalty or promptness. List ten or more values your super hero/shero will consider important. Rank these on a scale of one to ten, ten being the most important value and one being the least important.

                                VALUE   **RANK**

1. _____ _____
2. _____ _____
3. _____ _____
4. _____ _____
5. _____ _____
6. _____ _____
7. _____ _____
8. _____ _____
9. _____ _____
10. _____ _____

Look at the four highest ranked values. How will the valuing of these qualities affect the behavior of your super hero/shero?

Value Ranked 10: _____

_____

Value Ranked 9: _____

_____

Value Ranked 8: _____

_____

Value Ranked 7: _____

Educational Impressions, Inc.   *Create Heroes and Villains*

Tools of the Trade

Activity No. 5 **Teacher Directions**

Objectives: To involve students in analyzing the uses of various kinds of tools and equipment used by super heroes/sheroes

To assist students in projecting the outcome of ideas

To provide an opportunity for students to invent special tools and equipment for their super heroes/sheroes

Thinking Skills: Recall

Application

Divergent Thinking

Synthesis

Directions: Discuss the following: What special tools and/or equipment does your favorite super hero/shero use? Explain. Where are they kept when not in use? How does your favorite super hero/shero get to them when they are needed?

Establish the fact that for a tool or a special piece of equipment to be useful, it must be available at the time it is needed and it must be in perfect working order. Have students fill out Activity No. 5 individually. Stress the fact that students should list only their original ideas; they should not borrow them from an already-created super hero/shero. Then have students share their ideas with the class.

Options: Simple everyday materials which can be substituted for more advanced, more sophisticated hardware

How tools are useful

Man's first tools

Tools of the Trade

Activity No. 5　　　　　　　　　　　　　　　　　　　　**Student Work Sheet**

In addition to having super powers, super heroes/sheroes often use special tools and equipment, such as Wonder Woman's lasso, bracelets and crown. Sometimes these tools themselves are endowed with magical qualities; sometimes they are simply tools used to achieve a goal. Create special tools and equipment for your super hero/shero. How will each tool be used? Where will it be kept when it is not in use? Remember, it must be at hand when needed.

1. _____

2. _____

3. _____

4. _____

5. _____

Educational Impressions, Inc.　　　　　　　　　　　　　　*Create Heroes and Villains*

Strengths and Weaknesses

Activity No. 6 **Teacher Directions**

Objectives:
To encourage students to examine various kinds of strengths and weaknesses—physical, mental, and moral—and to make comparisons

To provoke students to look beneath the surface in order to find hidden strengths and weaknesses

To guide students in creating special strengths and weaknesses for their super heroes/sheroes

Thinking Skills:
Recall

Application

Divergent Thinking

Synthesis

Evaluation

Directions:
Discuss the following: What special strengths and weaknesses does your favorite super hero/shero possess? Into what category do these strengths and weaknesses fall—physical, mental, or moral? Does he/she have strengths and weaknesses in more than one category? Explain. How do the strengths help your favorite super hero/shero? How do the weaknesses hinder him/her? How are the weaknesses used to create a story?

Arrive at a consensus of what "strength" and "weakness" mean. Next define "strength" and "weakness" in terms of physical, mental, moral, and other categories which students may suggest. Direct students to fill out Activity No. 6 individually. Then have them share their choices, explaining the reasons for them and their possible consequences.

Options:
Famous "strong" men/women

Fictional "weak" characters

Why people admire strength and abhor weakness

22 *Create Heroes and Villains* **Educational Impressions, Inc.**

Strengths and Weaknesses

Activity No. 6   **Student Work Sheet**

In Activity No. 2 you created special powers for your super hero/shero. These special powers can be looked at as strengths. In addition to the special powers your super hero/shero possesses, what are some very human strengths which he/she might have? What contributions could these strengths make?

	Strengths	**Contributions**
1.	_____	_____
2.	_____	_____
3.	_____	_____
4.	_____	_____

Super heroes/sheroes also have special weaknesses—physical, mental, or moral—of which their opponents are quick to take advantage. Superman's weakness from kryptonite is an example. What weaknesses might your super hero/shero possess? What problems could each weakness cause?

	Strengths	**Problems**
1.	_____	_____
2.	_____	_____
3.	_____	_____
4.	_____	_____

Problems and Crises

Activity No. 7 **Teacher Directions**

Objectives: To promote an understanding that a super hero/shero must have a crisis, conflict, or problem with which to deal; otherwise, there can be no story

To engage students in thinking about problems and how to solve them

To motivate students to create crisis situations which they will use later in creating their own stories

Thinking Skills: Recall

Application

Divergent Thinking

Convergent Thinking

Directions: Discuss the following: What is a crisis? What is a conflict? What is a problem? Are they the same? Why or why not? What does intervention mean? What kinds of crisis situations does your favorite super hero/shero encounter? How does he/she deal with crisis situations?

Make sure that students understand that problems are necessary; otherwise, there could be no stories. Fill in the top half of Activity No. 7 as a group, discussing each suggestion. Next have students fill in the bottom half of Activity No. 7 individually. After students have finished, have them share with the group. Discuss whether or not the problems/crises they listed would work in a story.

Options: Personal problems and ways of dealing with them

Ways to help others deal with problems

Problems and Crises

Activity No. 7 **Student Work Sheet**

Without something to correct or make better, super heroes/sheroes would not exist. They need crisis situations, conflicts, or problems which require their intervention.

Super Heroes/Sheroes **Situations**

1. _____ _____

_____

2. _____ _____

_____

3. _____ _____

_____

4. _____ _____

_____

5. _____ _____

What kinds of problems would your super hero/shero be likely to solve? From what kinds of crises would he/she rescue people?

1. _____

_____

2. _____

_____

3. _____

_____

4. _____

_____

5. _____

_____

Educational Impressions, Inc. *Create Heroes and Villains*

Super Villains

Activity No. 8 **Teacher Directions**

Objectives:
To guide students in understanding the importance of conflict in a story

To assist students in analyzing various kinds of conflict

To involve students in creating possible villains for their super heroes/sheroes

Thinking Skills:
Recall

Analysis

Divergent Thinking

Convergent Thinking

Synthesis

Evaluation

Directions:
Discuss the following: Who are some of the villains your favorite super hero/shero faces? What are they like? Does he/she face the same one(s) over and over? What could be the advantages to the writer of using the same villain again? To the reader? What could be the disadvantages?

Make sure that students understand that a well-drawn villain is just as important as a well-designed super hero/shero. The villain(s) must always be worthy of the super hero/shero. Have students create four possible villains. Then have them pick their best ones and discuss their choices. Tell them to hold the others for possible use later.

Options:
Conflict

Famous fictional villains

Infamous historical villains

Super Villains

Activity No. 8   **Student Work Sheet**

Some super heroes/sheroes face the same opponent(s), also called enemies, archenemies, foes, or villains, over and over again. Superman versus Lex Luther is an example. Others face their opponents only once. List below four possible opponents for your super hero/shero. Give the name, profession or occupation, some distinguishing physical and character traits, strengths, and weaknesses. What does the villain value most and why?

1. _____
   _____
   _____

2. _____
   _____
   _____

3. _____
   _____
   _____

4. _____
   _____
   _____

5. _____
   _____
   _____

Now go back and pick one villain who will be the major enemy of your super hero/shero. Why did you make that choice?

Villain: _____

Reason for choice: _____
_____
_____

Writing the Story

Activity No. 8 **Teacher Directions**

Objectives: To assist students in analyzing the parts of a short story

To aid students in the construction of a short story

To engage students in writing a short story

Thinking Skills: Analysis

Synthesis

Evaluation

Directions: Discuss the following: Why must a story have a beginning, a middle, and an end? What kinds of conflicts might your hero/shero encounter: man vs. man, man vs. fate, man vs. himself, man vs. aliens, or man vs. nature? How could he/she solve those conflicts? Why would a reader be more intrigued by the use of brains to solve a conflict as opposed to the use of brawn?

Instruct students to write their stories. They will probably prefer to use the third person and the past tense. Cover any writing mechanics which are necessary, such as the use of direct quotations, etc. After students have finished writing their stories, have them swap with each other for proofreading. After corrections have been made, ask students to share their stories aloud.

Options: Activity No. 10: Prepackaged Super Sheroes

Activity No. 21: Other Ways to Use a Hero

Activity No. 22: Group-Created Stories

Writing the Story

Activity No. 9

Student Work Sheet

Based upon all the information which you have compiled on your super hero/shero, write a short story detailing how your super hero/shero became super and what happened because of becoming super. Treat this short story as the first in a series of exciting adventures. Remember, a short story occurs in three parts:

1. The beginning where the characters and situation(s) are introduced,

2. The middle where complications arise (a series of complications, problems, or conflicts may be encountered here), and

3. The ending where the complications are resolved.

If you intend to use your villain again, you must leave him/her alive at the end in a situation which temporarily resolves the complications, but which leaves him/her capable of causing mischief again. Use direct conversation and show action as it happens rather than as an accomplished fact. If possible, solve conflicts without resorting to undue violence. Readers admire heroes/sheroes who are able to use brains as well as brawn.

When you finish writing your story, swap with a classmate. Proofread each other's stories and then correct all errors.

You might like to make copies of your stories and bind them into a magazine.

Prepackaged Super Sheroes

Activity No. 10   **Teacher Directions**

Objectives: To provide already-created super sheroes as a means of getting started in the creative process

To provide more opportunities for those students who wish to continue writing stories using super heroes/sheroes

Thinking Skills: Observation

Analysis

Convergent Thinking

Divergent Thinking

Synthesis

Evaluation

Directions: Read the brief descriptions of Super Granny and Orangutana aloud. Discuss the following: In what kinds of believable situations would Super Granny or Orangutana find themselves? How would they cope? How will the age, sex, physical appearance, peculiarities, and values of Super Granny and Orangutana influence how they will respond to people and how people will respond to them? How will these factors influence how they will respond to crisis situations?

Have students pick either Super Granny or Orangutana as the main character in a story. Assist them in preparing an outline for that story. Then have them write their stories. Ask them to share them orally.

Options: Activity No. 21: Other Ways to Use a Hero

Activity No. 22: Group-Created Stories

Prepackaged Super Sheroes

Activity No. 10 **Student Work Sheet**

You might like to use one of the following super sheroes as the main character in a story or as a cohort for your own created super hero/shero.

Super Granny* is a small, frail-appearing grandmother whose undercover name is Mary Marshall. She is the typical grandmother, baking cookies for her grandchildren and taking care of her numerous cats. But—whenever a child is in any danger, Super Granny emerges. She whips off her apron, turns it inside out, ties it around her neck, and presto—it becomes a magic cape with the symbol SG on the back! Her glasses, her necklace watch, her hearing aid, her cameo brooch, her umbrella, her pocketbook, and her shoes all hold special surprises for any super villain who plans to harm a child. (You provide the surprises.) Super Granny has only one weakness—without her glasses she can see only two feet in front of her.

Orangutana* is a young, beautiful, blue-eyed blonde female who is 5'7" tall and is known as Lori Landers. She is a student of pithecology, the study of apes. One day she was bitten by a radioactive flea which had just bitten her favorite orangutan, Sheba. From that point on, Lori has had super strength whenever a primate is in danger. As soon as she senses danger to any primate, she begins to change. She grows taller and broader; her arms lengthen; her senses become super sharp; she becomes brilliantly cunning; and her strength becomes that of a dozen orangutans. She uses no special tools, but makes cunning use of any material which is handy. She does have an inordinate craving for bananas, set off by the smell of the fruit. When the craving hits, she **must** stop whatever she is doing and eat a banana.

*Created by students in the Heard County, Georgia, Gifted Program

Definition of Folk Hero

Activity No. 11 **Teacher Directions**

Objectives: To help students arrive at a working definition of folk hero

To encourage students to analyze the folk heroes/sheroes they know

To help students to analyze the deeds performed by folk heroes/sheroes

To guide students in thinking of deeds their created folk heroes/sheroes might perform

Thinking Skills: Observation

Recall

Analysis

Convergent Thinking

Divergent Thinking

Synthesis

Directions: Read and discuss the definition of folk hero.

Discuss the following: Who are your favorite folk heroes/sheroes? (Annie Christmas*, Joe Magarac, John Henry, Snake McGhee, Paul Bunyan, Pecos Bill, Alfred Bulltop Stormalong, Davy Crockett*, Buffalo Bill*, and Kit Carson*, are a few who might be discussed.) What daring feats did they perform? Why do we still read about them? What appeal do they have for the modern person? Why? Which ones actually lived? (See note below.)

Have students fill out the top half of Activity No. 11 together, discussing answers as students supply them. Then have them fill out the bottom half individually. Ask them to share their results.

Options: The differences in the way super heroes/sheroes are invented and the way folk heroes/sheroes develop

*Actually lived, but have become legendized

32 *Create Heroes and Villains* Educational Impressions, Inc.

Definition of Folk Hero

Activity No. 11

Student Work Sheet

Folk heroes/sheroes represent the common working-class people. They are of two types: those that have actually lived, but have become folk heroes/sheroes through repeated exaggeration and those that are completely fictional. Examples of those who actually lived include Davy Crockett and Annie Christmas. Examples of those that are completely fictional include Pecos Bill and Paul Bunyon. American folk heroes/sheroes are usually wise and wonderful, larger than life in both size and heart, always human, and very often warmly humorous. They reveal American traditions and aspirations and give eternal hope that life and people can become a little better than they are at present. Below list some folk heroes/sheroes and some of the deeds they have performed.

Folk Heroes/Sheroes   **Deeds**

1. _____   _____
                                   _____

2. _____   _____
                                   _____

3. _____   _____
                                   _____

4. _____   _____
                                   _____

5. _____   _____

What deeds will your created folk hero/shero perform?

_____
_____
_____
_____
_____
_____

Occupations and Values

Activity No. 12 **Teacher Directions**

Objectives: To encourage students to analyze the occupations held by folk heroes/sheroes and to help them to understand the value and importance of work

To provide an atmosphere wherein students may openly examine and discuss values

To encourage students to reason and project the consequences of certain choices

To engage students in developing occupations and values for their folk heroes/sheroes

Thinking Skills: Application

Analysis

Convergent Thinking

Divergent Thinking

Synthesis

Evaluation

Directions: Discuss the following: Why is the occupation held by a folk hero/shero important? What kinds of things would certain occupations allow a folk hero/shero to do?

Have students fill out the top part of Activity No. 12 individually. Then have them discuss their choices and reasons.

Discuss the following: What are some of the values held by your favorite folk hero/shero? How do the values held by your favorite folk hero/shero affect the decisions made by him/her?

Guide students in understanding that what people value determines the decisions they make and the actions they take. Have the students fill out the bottom part of Activity No. 12. Have them share what they wrote.

Options: Blue-collar jobs

Occupations and Values

Activity No. 12 **Student Work Sheet**

Folk heroes/sheroes are almost always closely allied with their occupations, occupations which are very active and require extraordinary strength, spirit, and stamina. John Henry was a "steel-driving" man, working on railroads. Annie Christmas was a lady longshoreman, working on the docks in New Orleans. Joe Magarac worked in the steel mills. Snake McGhee worked in the oil fields. Paul Bunyan was a lumberjack. Pecos Bill was a cowboy. Alfred Bulltop Stormalong was a sailor-whaler. Choose a modern-day occupation for your folk hero/shero. Choose one that gives your modern-day folk hero/shero a chance to be active and to perform brave, daring, and arduous deeds. Below describe the chosen occupation for your folk hero/shero. Why do you choose that one? How will it give your folk hero/shero a chance to be a hero/shero?

_____
_____
_____
_____
_____
_____
_____
_____
_____
_____

The values folk heroes/sheroes hold are those held by the class of people they represent; however, generally the values held by the folk hero/shero are stronger and adhered to more strictly. Which values will your folk hero/shero hold? (See Activity No. 4.) How will these values affect his/her actions?

_____
_____
_____
_____
_____
_____

Educational Impressions, Inc.   Create Heroes and Villains

Characteristics

Activity No. 13 **Teacher Directions**

Objectives:
To assist students in understanding factors which make up the total person

To provoke students to question initial reactions to people based on superficial qualities

To assist students in selecting the component parts for their folk heroes/sheroes

Thinking Skills:
Recall

Application

Analysis

Synthesis

Evaluation

Directions:
Discuss the following: What sex, ethnic background, and age of your favorite folk hero/shero? What is his/her personality like? In what ways do sex, ethnic background, age, and personality affect what your folk hero/shero does? How do the sex, ethnic background, age and personality of your favorite folk hero/shero affect the way other characters respond to him/her? How do they affect the way you as a reader respond to him/her?

Lead students to an understanding of how various characteristics have either positive or negative effects and that not all people view a given characteristic in the same light. Have students fill in Activity No. 13 individually, giving special thought to each item. Then ask students to share their work, giving reasons for each choice.

Options:
Stereotypes

Minority folk heroes/sheroes

Characteristics

Activity No. 13 **Student Work Sheet**

The sex, age, ethnic background, dress, geographical origin, occupation, values, size and shape, personality, and name help determine how a folk hero/shero behaves, how other characters respond to him/her, and how a reader responds to him/her. Think through what you want your folk hero/shero to be or do before you determine each factor listed below.

Name _____

Age _____

Sex _____

Ethnic Background _____

Physical Appearance:

    Height _____

    Weight _____

    Build _____

    Skin tone _____

    Hair color _____

    Eye color _____

    Other _____

Likes _____

_____

_____

Dislikes _____

_____

_____

Dress _____

_____

_____

Personality _____

_____

_____

Educational Impressions, Inc.

Strengths and Weaknesses

Activity No. 14

Teacher Directions

Objectives:
To encourage students to examine various kinds of strengths and weaknesses—physical, mental, and moral—and to make comparisons

To provoke students to look beneath the surface in order to find hidden strengths and weaknesses

To guide students in creating special strengths and weaknesses for their folk heroes/sheroes

Thinking Skills:
Recall

Application

Divergent Thinking

Synthesis

Evaluation

Directions:
Discuss the following: What special strengths (weaknesses) does your favorite folk hero/shero possess? Into which category do these strengths (weaknesses) fall—mental, moral or physical? Does he/she have strengths (weaknesses) in more than one category? Explain. How do these strengths help your favorite folk hero/shero? How are the weaknesses used in creating a story?

Arrive at a consensus of what "strength" and "weakness" mean. Next define "strength" and "weakness" in terms of physical, mental, moral, and any other category which students may suggest. Direct students to fill out Activity No. 14 individually. Then have them share their choices and the possible consequences of their choices.

Options:
Special strengths developed by disabled people

Strengths and Weaknesses

Activity No. 14

Student Work Sheet

Folk heroes/sheroes usually possess special strengths—physical, mental, or moral. What special strengths might your created folk hero/shero possess? How could these abilities contribute to the successes of your folk hero/shero?

       Strengths   **Contributions**

1. _____   _____

2. _____   _____

3. _____   _____

4. _____   _____

Folk heroes/sheroes also have special weaknesses—physical, mental, or moral—which lead to complications. What weaknesses might your folk hero/shero possess? How might they contribute to the problems your folk hero/shero faces?

       Strengths   **Problems**

1. _____   _____

2. _____   _____

3. _____   _____

4. _____   _____

Now choose two strengths and two weaknesses from the lists above. Pair these strengths and weaknesses to create balance. How can they balance each other in your story?

Villains

Activity No. 15 **Teacher Directions**

Objectives:
To guide students in understanding the importance of conflict in a story

To assist students in analyzing various kinds of conflict

To involve students in creating possible villains for their folk heroes/sheroes

Thinking Skills:
Recall

Analysis

Divergent Thinking

Convergent Thinking

Synthesis

Evaluation

Directions:
Discuss the following: What is a natural disaster? What is progress? What is a hardship? What is a bully? Why might these be considered "villains" for folk heroes/sheroes? How might folk heroes/sheroes deal with each kind of "villain"?

Assist students in creating their bullies. Stress the fact that humor and exaggeration will contribute to the interest of the character. Next have students work out a logical way their folk hero/shero will deal with the bully. Have them share their ideas.

Options:
Have students create hardships and/or some form of progress with which to confront their folk heroes/sheroes. Ask them to verbalize how their folk hero/shero will cope.

Villains

Activity No. 15   **Student Work Sheet**

Folk heroes/sheroes face different "villains." Their "villains" are generally in the form of natural disasters (floods, storms, fires, hard freezes, earthquakes, and so on), progress (machines, technology, encroaching civilization, and so on), hardships, or bullies. Sometimes no "villains" are faced; instead, the folk hero/shero will perform great feats, such as digging the Grand Canyon or creating the Rocky Mountains. Below create a bully and a natural disaster for your folk hero/shero to face.

Bully: (You may wish to draw your bully on the back of this sheet.)

    Name _____ Age _____

    Sex _____ Ethnic Background _____

    Size and shape _____

    Personality _____

    _____

    _____

    Other characteristics _____

    _____

    How will your folk hero/shero deal with your bully? _____

    _____

    _____

    _____

Natural Disaster

    Type of disaster _____

    How will your folk hero/shero deal with the natural disaster? _____

    _____

    _____

    _____

Educational Impressions, Inc.   *Create Heroes and Villains*

Using Humor: Writing Tall Tales

Activity No. 16 **Teacher Directions**

Objectives: To assist students in understanding and analyzing the tall tales

To aid students in the construction of a tall tale

To engage students in the writing of a tall tale

Thinking Skills Analysis

Divergent Thinking

Convergent Thinking

Synthesis

Evaluation

Directions: Read at least one tall tale aloud to the students. Discuss the construction of the tale, what makes it humorous, and the characters.

Read the description of a tall tale at the top of Activity No. 16 and discuss it. Encourage students to make outlines of their tall tales before they start the actual writing. Ask them to share their work.

Options: Students might like to use the "frame technique," a story within a story, when writing their tall tales. Sometimes writers of tall tales about folk heroes/sheroes utilize the "frame technique" in writing their tales. When this technique is used, the writer introduces a conventional narrator, who then describes the "real" teller of the tale and makes appropriate comments as the tale progresses. Appropriate language is used by the narrator, the "real" teller of the tale, and the characters of the tale. The character and idiom contrast add to the humor of the tale. Both tales are well planned and build up to a startling ending. No moral or postscript is used.

Activity No. 17: Suzy Stacks, A Trucking Shero

Using Humor: Writing Tall Tales

Activity No. 16 **Student Work Sheet**

Folk heroes/sheroes are often found in tall tales. Tall tales are imaginative, humorous, and exaggerated. Facts are stretched to the point of absurdity, thus tall tales become combinations of fact and impossibility. The tall tale is told deadpan; the narrator never shows amusement or disbelief. Details and accuracy are used to build up the narrator's credibility—then little by little the "lying" starts, building up to the biggest "lie," the "whopper" at the end. Using your created folk hero/shero and the special "villains" you created for him/her, write your tall tale. Pick a title that is appropriate, one that will catch the reader's interest. Remember, a good tall tale has three parts:

1. The beginning where the characters and situation(s) are introduced and the "truth" is told,

2. The middle where "stretching the truth" starts and where complications arise and are dealt with humorously, building up to

3. The ending, which is brief and often the biggest "lie" in a series of "lies."

Use direct conversation and show action as it happens rather than as accomplished fact. If possible, resolve conflicts without resorting to undue violence. Use cunning and trickery, spiced with humor, to solve problems whenever possible.

When you finish writing your story, swap with a classmate. Proofread each other's stories and then correct all errors.

You might want to copy the stories and bind them together. Perhaps the class would like to present the tall tales to other classes and/or to parents.

Suzy Stacks: A Trucking Shero

Activity No. 17   **Teacher Directions**

Objectives:	To provide an already-created folk shero as a means of getting students started in the creative process
	To provide more opportunities for those students who wish to continue writing stories using folk heroes/sheroes
Thinking Skills:	Observation
	Analysis
	Divergent Thinking
	Convergent Thinking
	Synthesis
	Evaluation
Directions:	Read the description of Suzy Stacks. Discuss the following: In what kinds of believable situations would Suzy find herself? How would she cope? How will the age, sex, physical appearance, peculiarities, and values of Suzy influence how she will respond to people and how people will respond to her? How will these factors influence how she will respond to crisis situations?
	Assist students in preparing an outline of a story using Suzy as the main character. Then have them write their stories. Ask them to share their stories with their classmates.
Options:	Assist students in writing story starters using Suzy Stacks and Crazy Charlie. Put them in a box and mix them well. Pass the box of story starters around the classroom and have the students pick one out of the box at random.
	Activity No. 21
	Activity No. 22
	Activity No. 23

44 *Create Heroes and Villains*   Educational Impressions, Inc.

Suzy Stacks: A Trucking Shero

Activity No. 17   **Student Work Sheet**

Suzy Stacks is beautiful. She is six-feet tall and has flaming red hair, piercing green eyes, and freckles. She is slender, but has amazing strength. She is an independent truck driver, willing and able to drive anywhere in the world. She is honest and intelligent and always delivers her load on time and in perfect condition. Her cat, Eighteen Wheels, accompanies her on all her trips. Suzy drives a custom-built Kenworth with a cat symbol on the door. Her CB handle is Cat Eyes. Suzy has a fondness for country music; blonde, brown-eyed cowboys; rodeos; Charles Dickens; and fried chicken. She wears silk shirts with her denim jeans, designer boots, and an emerald ring, which she inherited from her Grandmother Stacks. Her nemeses are bad weather, bad roads, mechanical drivers, and Crazy Charlie. Crazy Charlie thinks all females should stay at home. He will do **anything** to discredit Suzy.

You might want to use Suzy in one of these situations:

Crazy Charlie is out to get Suzy again. He is spreading the word that she is hauling "dope." He plans to plant some in Suzy's truck. Write a story showing how Suzy outsmarts Crazy Charlie.

Crazy Charlie has hired an actor to help him steal Eighteen Wheels. He plans to use Eighteen Wheels as a "clue" to implicate Suzy in a crime he is planning. The actor has bleached his hair blonde and is wearing contact lenses to make his eyes appear brown. He is pretending to be a rodeo cowboy so he can strike up an acquaintance with Suzy. How will Suzy discover the plot laid against her? How will she recover Eighteen Wheels? How will she clear her name? Write a tall tale that includes the answers to these questions.

The Mythological Hero

Activity No. 18

Teacher Directions

Objectives: To promote an understanding of what a mythological hero is

To provide an opportunity to study and analyze Greek and Roman heroes and to analyze the adventures of mythological heroes

To involve students in creating a mythological hero/heroine

Thinking Skills: Observation

Recall

Application

Analysis

Divergent Thinking

Convergent Thinking

Synthesis

Directions: Read aloud one or two Greek or Roman myths featuring mythological heroes/heroines. Analyze them.

Read the introduction to Activity No. 18. Discuss each part of the description of a mythological hero.

Before directing students to write, stress the fact that originally myths and tales were spread orally, but that they will be creating a hero for an ancient time and a foreign place. To help make their stories more authentic, encourage students to make use of Greek or Roman gods, goddesses, and places.

Discuss the questions that students will answer in creating a mythological hero/heroine. Add other questions if the need arises. Have students create their own heroes/heroines using the questions as a guide. Ask them to share their creations orally.

Options: Greek and Roman gods and goddesses

Creation myths

The Mythological Hero

Activity No. 18 **Student Work Sheet**

Hero adventure myths or tales have certain well-defined characteristics. They describe the adventures of human beings who transcend ordinary men by their strength, courage, intelligence, and skill. They value honor, courage, strength, and generosity. They excel in war and adventure. Sometimes they possess supernatural powers and are often helped by gods, goddesses, or special magic. They battle monsters and demons and their journeys are not always confined to this world. They are often the result of the union of a god or goddess and a mortal; they themselves are usually mortal. (Heracles [Hercules] was the son of Zeus and the mortal Alcmene.) Create a mythological hero/heroine using the Greek and Roman heroes/heroines as models. Keep in mind the following questions as you work on your creation:

1. What is the name of your hero/heroine?

2. What kind of appearance and personality does he/she have?

3. What is the origin of your hero/heroine?

4. What makes him/her a hero/heroine?

5. What does he/she value? How do his/her values affect his/her behavior?

6. What special strengths does your hero/heroine possess? How do they help him/her?

7. Does he/she possess any magical powers? If so, how are they used? How did he/she get them?

8. What weaknesses does your hero/heroine possess? How do they hinder him/her?

9. Do any gods and/or goddesses help your hero/heroine? If so, which ones? Why? Under what circumstances?

10. What are some adventures your hero/heroine might have? Where do they take place?

11. What kind of journey might your hero/heroine undertake?

The Monster as Villain

Activity No. 19 **Teacher Directions**

Objectives: To help students gain an understanding of the characteristics of monsters

To guide students in the creation of monsters for their created mythological heroes/heroines to battle

Thinking Skills: Observation

Recall

Application

Analysis

Divergent Thinking

Convergent Thinking

Synthesis

Directions: Tell students the following: A monster is an animal of strange or terrifying shape. It is usually very large, deformed, ugly, wicked, and cruel. Monsters are very useful creatures to writers because they make fascinating villains, which heroes may battle and vanquish. In Greek and Roman mythology, monsters were often hybrids: the Chimera had the head and front of a lion, the body of a goat, and the hindquarter of a dragon; the Minotaur had a human body and the head and tail of a bull. Some other monsters which Greek and Roman heroes encountered include Argus, Cerberus, Cetus, the Cyclops, Geryon, the Gorgon Sisters (Stheno, Euryale, and Medusa), the Harpies, and the Hydra.

Read the introduction to Activity No. 19. Assist students in drawing labeling, and describing their monsters. Make sure they answer the related questions. Ask them to share their work with the class.

Options: Good vs. evil as a literary theme

Conflict

The Monster as Villain

Activity No. 19

Student Work Sheet

Mythological heroes very often had to conquer villains in the form of monsters. Perseus removed Medusa's head. Theseus slew the Minotaur. Heracles (Hercules) overcame many monsters in his Twelve Labors. (Look them up.) In the space below draw a monster for your mythological hero/heroine to battle. Label and describe it.

Answer the following questions about your monster:

1. When and why did the monster come into being?

2. Who has already tried to destroy it? Why wasn't it conquered?

3. What terrible things has it done? To whom and/or to what did it do them?

Write a Heroic Tale

Activity No. 20   **Teacher Directions**

Objectives: To assist student in analyzing the parts of heroic myths

To aid students in the construction of a heroic myth

To engage students in writing a heroic myth

Thinking Skills: Observation

Recall

Application

Analysis

Synthesis

Directions: Tell students the following: Mythological heroes usually go on a journey. The story itself is in three main parts: The first part introduces the hero and the need for the journey. The second part is the journey itself, where the hero is usually helped by divine intervention or supernatural powers. The hero will meet various interesting characters along the way; these characters will either help or hinder him. Finally, he will reach his destination and achieve his goal. In the third part the hero will return for praise, glory, and reward.

Read the introduction to Activity No. 20. Discuss the questions with the students. Add other questions if needed. Help students make outlines for their stories. Check the outlines. Then have the students write their stories. Ask them to share their stories with the class.

Options: Activity No. 21

Activity No. 22

Activity No. 23

Write a Heroic Tale

Activity No. 20

Student Work Sheet

Using the mythological hero/heroine which you created in Activity No. 18 and the monster you created in Activity No. 19, write an adventure story featuring the two. Include the information you have already created. Answer the following questions in detail in writing your story. Rearrange the order of the questions to suit your own individual story.

1. Who is your hero/heroine?
2. What is he/she like?
3. Who or what causes him/her to start a journey?
4. What is the purpose of the journey?
5. From where does he/she start?
6. What happens along the way?
7. Where does he/she go?
8. To what place does he/she return?
9. What gods, goddesses, and/or other supernatural beings help your hero/heroine?
10. Why and how do the supernatural beings help him/her?
11. What is the monster? What terrible things has it done?
12. Do any other monsters and/or obstacles stand in his/her way?
13. Who has tried unsuccessfully to destroy the monster or to render it harmless?
14. Under what circumstances did the others try? Why did they fail?
15. What happens when your hero/heroine and the monster meet?
16. What happens last? How does the story end?

Use direct conversation, showing the action as it occurs. Describe the characters in detail; be sure to include their thoughts, feelings, actions, and reactions. Describe the setting. Work bits and pieces of the information into the story as it progresses.

Educational Impressions, Inc.

Other Ways to Use a Hero

Activity Nos. 21, 22, and 23  **Teacher Directions**

Objectives: To provide opportunities for those students who wish to continue writing stories using heroes/heroines

Thinking Skills: Observation

Recall

Application

Analysis

Divergent Thinking

Convergent Thinking

Synthesis

Evaluation

Directions: These three activities can be used to extend the **Create Heroes and Villains** teaching unit as follow-ups at later dates during the year, before starting Activity No. 1, or individually as one-shot writing assignments. No individual teacher directions are given; instead, the student pages are fairly complete by themselves.

Activity No. 21: Other Ways to Use a Hero

Activity No. 22: Group-Created Stores

Activity No. 23: A Grab Bag of Suggestions

Other Ways to Use a Hero

Activity No. 21  **Student Work Sheet**

In addition to writing a short story using your created heroes/heroines, you may wish to try some of the following suggestions:

Write a radio script. With appropriate sound effects, the script may be produced for an audience by simply using a screen to conceal the participants from their audience. The script could also be recorded on a tape recorder and then played for the audience. Don't overlook the use of music to achieve startling effects.

Write a play. A play is not complete unless it is staged. Producing a play involves more work than producing a radio show because the audience sees the actors. Lines and actions must be learned; whereas, in a radio show the lines can be read. If you have access to a video camera, filming the play could be an interesting experience.

Draw a comic strip. Study a comic book first so you are thoroughly familiar with all the conventions of comic-book writing.

Write a narrative poem. Treat your hero/heroine as either an epic hero/heroine.

Write a song. Set it to music and record it on a tape recorder.

Draw a filmstrip of the story you wrote in Activity No. 9, Activity No. 16, or Activity No. 20; or write a new story. Record the story on a tape recorder and synchronize the two to show to an audience.

Draw cartoons of all your created heroes/heroines. Show them in situations which reveal their true personalities and characters.

Write a story where your folk hero/shero, your super hero/shero, and your mythological hero/heroine combine their talents to "save mankind." Come up with some ideas to make the story plausible, such as having it happen in a dream.

Group-Created Stories

Activity No. 22

Student Work Sheet

Using the basic characteristics learned in the preceding activities, create group stories using the following process:

Divide into small groups. Four students per group is recommended.

Each member of the group will select one of the following tasks and will complete the assignment individually:

1. Create a super hero/shero, a folk hero/shero, or a mythological hero/heroine.
2. Create a super villain, a bully, or a monster.
3. Create a setting and a basic situation.
4. Create a crisis, one or more conflicts, and complications.

After you have completed the above assignment individually, return to your group. Now put your imaginations to work. Using the materials you have created, write one of the following:

1. A short story
2. A radio script
3. A play
4. A poem
5. A song
6. A comic strip
7. A filmstrip
8. A cartoon

See Activity No. 21 for suggestions on how to create these products.

Using your created super hero/shero, mythological hero/heroine, and/or folk hero/heroine and the same kind of hero/heroine created by a classmate, co-author with that classmate a story wherein both your heroes/heroines star.

Write a Heroic Tale

Activity No. 20

Student Work Sheet

Using the mythological hero/heroine which you created in Activity No. 18 and the monster you created in Activity No. 19, write an adventure story featuring the two. Include the information you have already created. Answer the following questions in detail in writing your story. Rearrange the order of the questions to suit your own individual story.

1. Who is your hero/heroine?
2. What is he/she like?
3. Who or what causes him/her to start a journey?
4. What is the purpose of the journey?
5. From where does he/she start?
6. What happens along the way?
7. Where does he/she go?
8. To what place does he/she return?
9. What gods, goddesses, and/or other supernatural beings help your hero/heroine?
10. Why and how do the supernatural beings help him/her?
11. What is the monster? What terrible things has it done?
12. Do any other monsters and/or obstacles stand in his/her way?
13. Who has tried unsuccessfully to destroy the monster or to render it harmless?
14. Under what circumstances did the others try? Why did they fail?
15. What happens when your hero/heroine and the monster meet?
16. What happens last? How does the story end?

Use direct conversation, showing the action as it occurs. Describe the characters in detail; be sure to include their thoughts, feelings, actions, and reactions. Describe the setting. Work bits and pieces of the information into the story as it progresses.

Other Ways to Use a Hero

Activity Nos. 21, 22, and 23

Teacher Directions

Objectives: To provide opportunities for those students who wish to continue writing stories using heroes/heroines

Thinking Skills: Observation

Recall

Application

Analysis

Divergent Thinking

Convergent Thinking

Synthesis

Evaluation

Directions: These three activities can be used to extend the **Create Heroes and Villains** teaching unit as follow-ups at later dates during the year, before starting Activity No. 1, or individually as one-shot writing assignments. No individual teacher directions are given; instead, the student pages are fairly complete by themselves.

Activity No. 21: Other Ways to Use a Hero

Activity No. 22: Group-Created Stores

Activity No. 23: A Grab Bag of Suggestions

A Grab Bag of Suggestions

Activity No. 23

Student Work Sheet

Friendship among heroes (Damon and Pythias or David and Jonathan) is the theme of some tales and legends. Create a myth, tale, or legend where the theme (main idea) is that of friendship. The story should show the value of true friendship.

Pick a legendary hero/heroine, such as Robin Hood, Maid Marian, William Tell, or King Arthur. Write an adventure story featuring your chosen legendary hero/heroine.

Who is your favorite hero/heroine—living or dead? Why do you admire the person? Write an essay convincing your classmates that this person is indeed worthy of being considered a hero/heroine.

Choose a biblical hero/heroine, such as David, Ruth, Samson, Moses, or Esther. Rewrite his/her adventures in the format of a children's book. Write it in such a way that a three- to five-year-old child could understand it. Appropriately illustrate it. Bind it and give it to a young relative or friend.

The romantic hero and the romantic heroine have analyzable characteristics and behave in analyzable ways. Using the basic format used to create a super hero/shero and a folk hero/shero, analyze the heroes/heroines in romantic fiction. After you have worked out a formula for creating a romantic hero or heroine, fill in the blanks. Remember to create characters as complete as possible. Then allow your created characters to behave as people would with these characteristics as you write your story. Keep in mind the three main parts of a story. (See Activity No. 9.)

The western hero—the cowboy—is often referred to as the strong, silent type. Create a western hero and write an adventure story featuring him/her.

Do you have a favorite daydream where you become a hero/heroine? If so, try turning your daydream into a story. (Read James Thurber's short story "The Secret Live of Walter Mitty.")

A Grab Bag of Suggestions

Activity No. 23  **Student Work Sheet**

Friendship among heroes (Damon and Pythias or David and Jonathan) is the theme of some tales and legends. Create a myth, tale, or legend where the theme (main idea) is that of friendship. The story should show the value of true friendship.

Pick a legendary hero/heroine, such as Robin Hood, Maid Marian, William Tell, or King Arthur. Write an adventure story featuring your chosen legendary hero/heroine.

Who is your favorite hero/heroine—living or dead? Why do you admire the person? Write an essay convincing your classmates that this person is indeed worthy of being considered a hero/heroine.

Choose a biblical hero/heroine, such as David, Ruth, Samson, Moses, or Esther. Rewrite his/her adventures in the format of a children's book. Write it in such a way that a three- to five-year-old child could understand it. Appropriately illustrate it. Bind it and give it to a young relative or friend.

The romantic hero and the romantic heroine have analyzable characteristics and behave in analyzable ways. Using the basic format used to create a super hero/shero and a folk hero/shero, analyze the heroes/heroines in romantic fiction. After you have worked out a formula for creating a romantic hero or heroine, fill in the blanks. Remember to create characters as complete as possible. Then allow your created characters to behave as people would with these characteristics as you write your story. Keep in mind the three main parts of a story. (See Activity No. 9.)

The western hero—the cowboy—is often referred to as the strong, silent type. Create a western hero and write an adventure story featuring him/her.

Do you have a favorite daydream where you become a hero/heroine? If so, try turning your daydream into a story. (Read James Thurber's short story "The Secret Live of Walter Mitty.")

TEAR-OUT REPRODUCIBLE STUDENT WORK PAGES

What Is a Hero?

Activity No. 1 **Student Work Sheet**

There are many definitions of hero and heroine. Some of the most commonly accepted are listed below:

1. A hero/heroine is a person admired for his/her achievements and outstanding character.

2. A hero/heroine is a person who shows great courage.

3. A hero/heroine is the main character in a dramatic or literary work.

4. A hero/heroine is the central figure in an event or historical period.

5. A hero/heroine is an illustrious warrior.

6. A hero/heroine is a mythological or legendary figure, often of half-divine descent, endowed with extraordinary strength and/or ability.

List heroes and heroines who fit the above definitions. Be able to defend your choices.

HEROES	HEROINES
_____	_____
_____	_____
_____	_____
_____	_____
_____	_____
_____	_____

Definition of Super Hero/Shero

Activity No. 2 **Student Work Sheet**

A super hero/shero is larger than life. He/she will usually be superior in many ways to the ordinary person. First of all, he/she must have at least one super power; sometimes he/she has several super powers. These super powers may be physical, mental, or moral. Whatever these super powers are, they must be used to benefit mankind! Below list six super powers that your created super hero/shero might possess. Think beyond the obvious physical powers. How can these powers be used to benefit mankind?

	POWER	**TYPE AND USES**
1.	_____	_____
2.	_____	_____
3.	_____	_____
4.	_____	_____
5.	_____	_____
6.	_____	_____

Now choose two of the above for your super hero/shero.

1. _____

2. _____

Explain why you chose those two.

1. _____

_____

2. _____

_____

Educational Impressions, Inc   Create Heroes and Villains 59

Characteristics

Activity No. 3

Student Work Sheet

The sex, age, ethnic background, religion, dress, geographical origin, looks, and even name of your super hero/shero determine how the public views him/her. These factors also help determine how the super hero/shero behaves. Think through what you want your super hero/shero to be or do before you determine each factor below.

Undercover name & occupation _____

Super hero/shero name _____

Age _____ Ethnic background _____

Religion _____

Geographical origin: _____

Looks:

    Height _____

    Weight _____

    Build _____

    Hair Color _____

    Eye Color _____

Everyday dress _____

_____

_____

Costume with symbol _____

_____

_____

Values

Activity No. 4 **Student Work Sheet**

Super heroes/sheroes hold certain values. A super hero/shero may value honesty or loyalty or promptness. List ten or more values your super hero/shero will consider important. Rank these on a scale of one to ten, ten being the most important value and one being the least important.

	VALUE	RANK
1.	_____	____
2.	_____	____
3.	_____	____
4.	_____	____
5.	_____	____
6.	_____	____
7.	_____	____
8.	_____	____
9.	_____	____
10.	_____	____

Look at the four highest ranked values. How will the valuing of these qualities affect the behavior of your super hero/shero?

Value Ranked 10: _____

Value Ranked 9: _____

Value Ranked 8: _____

Value Ranked 7: _____

Educational Impressions, Inc.

Tools of the Trade

Activity No. 5 **Student Work Sheet**

In addition to having super powers, super heroes/sheroes often use special tools and equipment, such as Wonder Woman's lasso, bracelets and crown. Sometimes these tools themselves are endowed with magical qualities; sometimes they are simply tools used to achieve a goal. Create special tools and equipment for your super hero/shero. How will each tool be used? Where will it be kept when it is not in use? Remember, it must be at hand when needed.

1. _____
_____
_____
_____

2. _____
_____
_____
_____

3. _____
_____
_____
_____

4. _____
_____
_____
_____

5. _____
_____
_____
_____

Strengths and Weaknesses

Activity No. 6   **Student Work Sheet**

In Activity No. 2 you created special powers for your super hero/shero. These special powers can be looked at as strengths. In addition to the special powers your super hero/shero possesses, what are some very human strengths which he/she might have? What contributions could these strengths make?

Strengths	Contributions
1. _____	_____
2. _____	_____
3. _____	_____
4. _____	_____

Super heroes/sheroes also have special weaknesses—physical, mental, or moral—of which their opponents are quick to take advantage. Superman's weakness from kryptonite is an example. What weaknesses might your super hero/shero possess? What problems could each weakness cause?

Strengths	Problems
1. _____	_____
2. _____	_____
3. _____	_____
4. _____	_____

Problems and Crises

Activity No. 7

Student Work Sheet

Without something to correct or make better, super heroes/sheroes would not exist. They need crisis situations, conflicts, or problems which require their intervention.

Super Heroes/Sheroes	**Situations**
1. _____	_____
2. _____	_____
3. _____	_____
4. _____	_____
5. _____	_____

What kinds of problems would your super hero/shero be likely to solve? From what kinds of crises would he/she rescue people?

1. _____
_____

2. _____
_____

3. _____
_____

4. _____
_____

5. _____
_____

Super Villains

Activity No. 8

Student Work Sheet

Some super heroes/sheroes face the same opponent(s), also called enemies, archenemies, foes, or villains, over and over again. Superman versus Lex Luther is an example. Others face their opponents only once. List below four possible opponents for your super hero/shero. Give the name, profession or occupation, some distinguishing physical and character traits, strengths, and weaknesses. What does the villain value most and why?

1. _____
_____
_____

2. _____
_____
_____

3. _____
_____
_____

4 _____
_____
_____

5. _____
_____
_____

Now go back and pick one villain who will be the major enemy of your super hero/shero. Why did you make that choice?

Villain: _____

Reason for choice: _____
_____
_____

Educational Impressions, Inc.   *Create Heroes and Villains* 65

Writing the Story

Activity No. 9

Student Work Sheet

Based upon all the information which you have compiled on your super hero/shero, write a short story detailing how your super hero/shero became super and what happened because of becoming super. Treat this short story as the first in a series of exciting adventures. Remember, a short story occurs in three parts:

1. The beginning where the characters and situation(s) are introduced,

2. The middle where complications arise (a series of complications, problems, or conflicts may be encountered here), and

3. The ending where the complications are resolved.

If you intend to use your villain again, you must leave him/her alive at the end in a situation which temporarily resolves the complications, but which leaves him/her capable of causing mischief again. Use direct conversation and show action as it happens rather than as an accomplished fact. If possible, solve conflicts without resorting to undue violence. Readers admire heroes/sheroes who are able to use brains as well as brawn.

When you finish writing your story, swap with a classmate. Proofread each other's stories and then correct all errors.

You might like to make copies of your stories and bind them into a magazine.

Prepackaged Super Sheroes

Activity No. 10

Student Work Sheet

You might like to use one of the following super sheroes as the main character in a story or as a cohort for your own created super hero/shero.

Super Granny* is a small, frail-appearing grandmother whose undercover name is Mary Marshall. She is the typical grandmother, baking cookies for her grandchildren and taking care of her numerous cats. But—whenever a child is in any danger, Super Granny emerges. She whips off her apron, turns it inside out, ties it around her neck, and presto—it becomes a magic cape with the symbol SG on the back! Her glasses, her necklace watch, her hearing aid, her cameo brooch, her umbrella, her pocketbook, and her shoes all hold special surprises for any super villain who plans to harm a child. (You provide the surprises.) Super Granny has only one weakness—without her glasses she can see only two feet in front of her.

Orangutana* is a young, beautiful, blue-eyed blonde female who is 5'7" tall and is known as Lori Landers. She is a student of pithecology, the study of apes. One day she was bitten by a radioactive flea which had just bitten her favorite orangutan, Sheba. From that point on, Lori has had super strength whenever a primate is in danger. As soon as she senses danger to any primate, she begins to change. She grows taller and broader; her arms lengthen; her senses become super sharp; she becomes brilliantly cunning; and her strength becomes that of a dozen orangutans. She uses no special tools, but makes cunning use of any material which is handy. She does have an inordinate craving for bananas, set off by the smell of the fruit. When the craving hits, she **must** stop whatever she is doing and eat a banana.

*Created by students in the Heard County, Georgia, Gifted Program

Definition of Folk Hero

Activity No. 11

Student Work Sheet

Folk heroes/sheroes represent the common working-class people. They are of two types: those that have actually lived, but have become folk heroes/sheroes through repeated exaggeration and those that are completely fictional. Examples of those who actually lived include Davy Crockett and Annie Christmas. Examples of those that are completely fictional include Pecos Bill and Paul Bunyon. American folk heroes/sheroes are usually wise and wonderful, larger than life in both size and heart, always human, and very often warmly humorous. They reveal American traditions and aspirations and give eternal hope that life and people can become a little better than they are at present. Below list some folk heroes/sheroes and some of the deeds they have performed.

Folk Heroes/Sheroes	**Deeds**
1. _____	_____
2. _____	_____
3. _____	_____
4. _____	_____
5. _____	_____

What deeds will your created folk hero/shero perform?

_____
_____
_____
_____
_____
_____

Occupations and Values

Activity No. 12

Student Work Sheet

Folk heroes/sheroes are almost always closely allied with their occupations, occupations which are very active and require extraordinary strength, spirit, and stamina. John Henry was a "steel-driving" man, working on railroads. Annie Christmas was a lady longshoreman, working on the docks in New Orleans. Joe Magarac worked in the steel mills. Snake McGhee worked in the oil fields. Paul Bunyan was a lumberjack. Pecos Bill was a cowboy. Alfred Bulltop Stormalong was a sailor-whaler. Choose a modern-day occupation for your folk hero/shero. Choose one that gives your modern-day folk hero/shero a chance to be active and to perform brave, daring, and arduous deeds. Below describe the chosen occupation for your folk hero/shero. Why do you choose that one? How will it give your folk hero/shero a chance to be a hero/shero?

_____

_____

_____

_____

_____

_____

_____

_____

_____

_____

The values folk heroes/sheroes hold are those held by the class of people they represent; however, generally the values held by the folk hero/shero are stronger and adhered to more strictly. Which values will your folk hero/shero hold? (See Activity No. 4.) How will these values affect his/her actions?

_____

_____

_____

_____

_____

Educational Impressions, Inc.

Create Heroes and Villains

Characteristics

Activity No. 13   **Student Work Sheet**

The sex, age, ethnic background, dress, geographical origin, occupation, values, size and shape, personality, and name help determine how a folk hero/shero behaves, how other characters respond to him/her, and how a reader responds to him/her. Think through what you want your folk hero/shero to be or do before you determine each factor listed below.

Name _____

Age _____

Sex _____

Ethnic Background _____

Physical Appearance:

    Height _____

    Weight _____

    Build _____

    Skin tone _____

    Hair color _____

    Eye color _____

    Other _____

Likes _____

_____

_____

Dislikes _____

_____

_____

Dress _____

_____

_____

Personality _____

_____

_____

Strengths and Weaknesses

Activity No. 14 **Student Work Sheet**

Folk heroes/sheroes usually possess special strengths—physical, mental, or moral. What special strengths might your created folk hero/shero possess? How could these abilities contribute to the successes of your folk hero/shero?

Strengths **Contributions**

1. _____ _____

2. _____ _____

3. _____ _____

4. _____ _____

Folk heroes/sheroes also have special weaknesses—physical, mental, or moral—which lead to complications. What weaknesses might your folk hero/shero possess? How might they contribute to the problems your folk hero/shero faces?

Strengths **Problems**

1. _____ _____

2. _____ _____

3. _____ _____

4. _____ _____

Now choose two strengths and two weaknesses from the lists above. Pair these strengths and weaknesses to create balance. How can they balance each other in your story?

_____

Educational Impressions, Inc. *Create Heroes and Villains* 71

Villains

Activity No. 15 **Student Work Sheet**

Folk heroes/sheroes face different "villains." Their "villains" are generally in the form of natural disasters (floods, storms, fires, hard freezes, earthquakes, and so on), progress (machines, technology, encroaching civilization, and so on), hardships, or bullies. Sometimes no "villains" are faced; instead, the folk hero/shero will perform great feats, such as digging the Grand Canyon or creating the Rocky Mountains. Below create a bully and a natural disaster for your folk hero/shero to face.

Bully: (You may wish to draw your bully on the back of this sheet.)

Name _____ Age _____

Sex _____ Ethnic Background _____

Size and shape _____

Personality _____

_____

_____

Other characteristics _____

_____

How will your folk hero/shero deal with your bully? _____

_____

_____

_____

Natural Disaster

Type of disaster _____

How will your folk hero/shero deal with the natural disaster? _____

_____

_____

_____

72 *Create Heroes and Villains* **Educational Impressions, Inc.**

Using Humor: Writing Tall Tales

Activity No. 16

Student Work Sheet

Folk heroes/sheroes are often found in tall tales. Tall tales are imaginative, humorous, and exaggerated. Facts are stretched to the point of absurdity, thus tall tales become combinations of fact and impossibility. The tall tale is told deadpan; the narrator never shows amusement or disbelief. Details and accuracy are used to build up the narrator's credibility—then little by little the "lying" starts, building up to the biggest "lie," the "whopper" at the end. Using your created folk hero/shero and the special "villains" you created for him/her, write your tall tale. Pick a title that is appropriate, one that will catch the reader's interest. Remember, a good tall tale has three parts:

1. The beginning where the characters and situation(s) are introduced and the "truth" is told,

2. The middle where "stretching the truth" starts and where complications arise and are dealt with humorously, building up to

3. The ending, which is brief and often the biggest "lie" in a series of "lies."

Use direct conversation and show action as it happens rather than as accomplished fact. If possible, resolve conflicts without resorting to undue violence. Use cunning and trickery, spiced with humor, to solve problems whenever possible.

When you finish writing your story, swap with a classmate. Proofread each other's stories and then correct all errors.

You might want to copy the stories and bind them together. Perhaps the class would like to present the tall tales to other classes and/or to parents.

Suzy Stacks: A Trucking Shero

Activity No. 17

Student Work Sheet

Suzy Stacks is beautiful. She is six-feet tall and has flaming red hair, piercing green eyes, and freckles. She is slender, but has amazing strength. She is an independent truck driver, willing and able to drive anywhere in the world. She is honest and intelligent and always delivers her load on time and in perfect condition. Her cat, Eighteen Wheels, accompanies her on all her trips. Suzy drives a custom-built Kenworth with a cat symbol on the door. Her CB handle is Cat Eyes. Suzy has a fondness for country music; blonde, brown-eyed cowboys; rodeos; Charles Dickens; and fried chicken. She wears silk shirts with her denim jeans, designer boots, and an emerald ring, which she inherited from her Grandmother Stacks. Her nemeses are bad weather, bad roads, mechanical drivers, and Crazy Charlie. Crazy Charlie thinks all females should stay at home. He will do **anything** to discredit Suzy.

You might want to use Suzy in one of these situations:

Crazy Charlie is out to get Suzy again. He is spreading the word that she is hauling "dope." He plans to plant some in Suzy's truck. Write a story showing how Suzy outsmarts Crazy Charlie.

Crazy Charlie has hired an actor to help him steal Eighteen Wheels. He plans to use Eighteen Wheels as a "clue" to implicate Suzy in a crime he is planning. The actor has bleached his hair blonde and is wearing contact lenses to make his eyes appear brown. He is pretending to be a rodeo cowboy so he can strike up an acquaintance with Suzy. How will Suzy discover the plot laid against her? How will she recover Eighteen Wheels? How will she clear her name? Write a tall tale that includes the answers to these questions.

Create Heroes and Villains — Educational Impressions, Inc.

The Mythological Hero

Activity No. 18 **Student Work Sheet**

Hero adventure myths or tales have certain well-defined characteristics. They describe the adventures of human beings who transcend ordinary men by their strength, courage, intelligence, and skill. They value honor, courage, strength, and generosity. They excel in war and adventure. Sometimes they possess supernatural powers and are often helped by gods, goddesses, or special magic. They battle monsters and demons and their journeys are not always confined to this world. They are often the result of the union of a god or goddess and a mortal; they themselves are usually mortal. (Heracles [Hercules] was the son of Zeus and the mortal Alcmene.) Create a mythological hero/heroine using the Greek and Roman heroes/heroines as models. Keep in mind the following questions as you work on your creation:

1. What is the name of your hero/heroine?

2. What kind of appearance and personality does he/she have?

3. What is the origin of your hero/heroine?

4. What makes him/her a hero/heroine?

5. What does he/she value? How do his/her values affect his/her behavior?

6. What special strengths does your hero/heroine possess? How do they help him/her?

7. Does he/she possess any magical powers? If so, how are they used? How did he/she get them?

8. What weaknesses does your hero/heroine possess? How do they hinder him/her?

9. Do any gods and/or goddesses help your hero/heroine? If so, which ones? Why? Under what circumstances?

10. What are some adventures your hero/heroine might have? Where do they take place?

11. What kind of journey might your hero/heroine undertake?

Educational Impressions, Inc. *Create Heroes and Villains* 75

The Monster as Villain

Activity No. 19

Student Work Sheet

Mythological heroes very often had to conquer villains in the form of monsters. Perseus removed Medusa's head. Theseus slew the Minotaur. Heracles (Hercules) overcame many monsters in his Twelve Labors. (Look them up.) In the space below draw a monster for your mythological hero/heroine to battle. Label and describe it.

Answer the following questions about your monster:

1. When and why did the monster come into being?

2. Who has already tried to destroy it? Why wasn't it conquered?

3. What terrible things has it done? To whom and/or to what did it do them?

Write a Heroic Tale

Activity No. 20

Student Work Sheet

Using the mythological hero/heroine which you created in Activity No. 18 and the monster you created in Activity No. 19, write an adventure story featuring the two. Include the information you have already created. Answer the following questions in detail in writing your story. Rearrange the order of the questions to suit your own individual story.

1. Who is your hero/heroine?
2. What is he/she like?
3. Who or what causes him/her to start a journey?
4. What is the purpose of the journey?
5. From where does he/she start?
6. What happens along the way?
7. Where does he/she go?
8. To what place does he/she return?
9. What gods, goddesses, and/or other supernatural beings help your hero/heroine?
10. Why and how do the supernatural beings help him/her?
11. What is the monster? What terrible things has it done?
12. Do any other monsters and/or obstacles stand in his/her way?
13. Who has tried unsuccessfully to destroy the monster or to render it harmless?
14. Under what circumstances did the others try? Why did they fail?
15. What happens when your hero/heroine and the monster meet?
16. What happens last? How does the story end?

Use direct conversation, showing the action as it occurs. Describe the characters in detail; be sure to include their thoughts, feelings, actions, and reactions. Describe the setting. Work bits and pieces of the information into the story as it progresses.

Other Ways to Use a Hero

Activity No. 21  Student Work Sheet

In addition to writing a short story using your created heroes/heroines, you may wish to try some of the following suggestions:

Write a radio script. With appropriate sound effects, the script may be produced for an audience by simply using a screen to conceal the participants from their audience. The script could also be recorded on a tape recorder and then played for the audience. Don't overlook the use of music to achieve startling effects.

Write a play. A play is not complete unless it is staged. Producing a play involves more work than producing a radio show because the audience sees the actors. Lines and actions must be learned; whereas, in a radio show the lines can be read. If you have access to a video camera, filming the play could be an interesting experience.

Draw a comic strip. Study a comic book first so you are thoroughly familiar with all the conventions of comic-book writing.

Write a narrative poem. Treat your hero/heroine as either an epic hero/heroine.

Write a song. Set it to music and record it on a tape recorder.

Draw a filmstrip of the story you wrote in Activity No. 9, Activity No. 16, or Activity No. 20; or write a new story. Record the story on a tape recorder and synchronize the two to show to an audience.

Draw cartoons of all your created heroes/heroines. Show them in situations which reveal their true personalities and characters.

Write a story where your folk hero/shero, your super hero/shero, and your mythological hero/heroine combine their talents to "save mankind." Come up with some ideas to make the story plausible, such as having it happen in a dream.

Group-Created Stories

Activity No. 22   **Student Work Sheet**

Using the basic characteristics learned in the preceding activities, create group stories using the following process:

Divide into small groups. Four students per group is recommended.

Each member of the group will select one of the following tasks and will complete the assignment individually:

1. Create a super hero/shero, a folk hero/shero, or a mythological hero/heroine.
2. Create a super villain, a bully, or a monster.
3. Create a setting and a basic situation.
4. Create a crisis, one or more conflicts, and complications.

After you have completed the above assignment individually, return to your group. Now put your imaginations to work. Using the materials you have created, write one of the following:

1. A short story
2. A radio script
3. A play
4. A poem
5. A song
6. A comic strip
7. A filmstrip
8. A cartoon

See Activity No. 21 for suggestions on how to create these products.

Using your created super hero/shero, mythological hero/heroine, and/or folk hero/heroine and the same kind of hero/heroine created by a classmate, co-author with that classmate a story wherein both your heroes/heroines star.

A Grab Bag of Suggestions

Activity No. 23  **Student Work Sheet**

Friendship among heroes (Damon and Pythias or David and Jonathan) is the theme of some tales and legends. Create a myth, tale, or legend where the theme (main idea) is that of friendship. The story should show the value of true friendship.

Pick a legendary hero/heroine, such as Robin Hood, Maid Marian, William Tell, or King Arthur. Write an adventure story featuring your chosen legendary hero/heroine.

Who is your favorite hero/heroine—living or dead? Why do you admire the person? Write an essay convincing your classmates that this person is indeed worthy of being considered a hero/heroine.

Choose a biblical hero/heroine, such as David, Ruth, Samson, Moses, or Esther. Rewrite his/her adventures in the format of a children's book. Write it in such a way that a three- to five-year-old child could understand it. Appropriately illustrate it. Bind it and give it to a young relative or friend.

The romantic hero and the romantic heroine have analyzable characteristics and behave in analyzable ways. Using the basic format used to create a super hero/shero and a folk hero/shero, analyze the heroes/heroines in romantic fiction. After you have worked out a formula for creating a romantic hero or heroine, fill in the blanks. Remember to create characters as complete as possible. Then allow your created characters to behave as people would with these characteristics as you write your story. Keep in mind the three main parts of a story. (See Activity No. 9.)

The western hero—the cowboy—is often referred to as the strong, silent type. Create a western hero and write an adventure story featuring him/her.

Do you have a favorite daydream where you become a hero/heroine? If so, try turning your daydream into a story. (Read James Thurber's short story "The Secret Live of Walter Mitty.")